GOODNIGHT COVINGTON

WRITTEN & ILLUSTRATED BY:

EMILY COOK

Summary: Watercolor illustrations and rhyming text bring back warm feelings and memories of Covington, Tennessee. The poetic rhythm of the story along with the soothing colors of the artwork will calm children before they go to sleep.

FIRST EDITION

FOR PAIGE AND TRIPP WHO'S STORIES
PROVED THE BIG HEART OF OUR SMALL TOWN.

FOR LUCY WHO SHOWED THE WORLD THAT
MIRACLES DO STILL HAPPEN AND HOW TO
LIVE A LIFE OF GRATITUDE AND GRACE.
GOLUCYGO.ORG

GOODNIGHT COURTHOUSE
& GAZEBO IN THE CENTER
OF OUR SQUARE.

GOODNIGHT CHURCHES
WHO'S BELLS REMIND
US THAT GOD IS
ALWAYS THERE.

GOODNIGHT LIBRARY
WITH ALL YOUR
BOOKS AND STORYTIME.

TIPTON COUNTY PUBLIC
LIBRARY

GOODNIGHT HISTORIC
DISTRICT WITH ALL
OF YOUR HOMES SO FINE.

MAIN
MAPLE

GOODNIGHT BOUTIQUES
ON THE SQUARE WITH
SO MANY THINGS
TO CHOOSE.

gorgeous!

GOODNIGHT TO
"THE LEADER"
BRINGING US
THE NEWS.

THE LEADER

THURSDAY, FEBRUARY 18, 2021   THE VOICE OF TIPTON COUNTY SINCE 1886

Goodnight, Tipton County!

Enjoy Your Snow Days!

It snowed 8-12 inches in Tipton County.

School children enjoyed the week out of the classroom sledding and making snowmen. Many families made snowcream.

Snowcream:
10-12 c of Fresh Snow
1 tsp of Vanilla Extract
1 can of Condensed Milk
Sprinkles Optional

Send us your best pictures of your snowman.

IN LIKE A LION
Neighborhood children squeal with joy as they sled around town.

Emily Cook Writes a Book

Local Author Emily Cook released her book "Eclectic Emily" with a book signing at Tipton Chr... Academy last Satu... Cook's second bo... "Goodnight Co... will release i... Cook also... illustrate... the bo...

GOODNIGHT RUFFIN
THEATRE WITH ALL OF
YOUR AMAZING PLAYS.

RUFFIN

GOODNIGHT
CANDY FACTORY
MAKING OUR
TOWN SMELL
SWEET EVERYDAY.

Candy
Candy
Candy

GOODNIGHT SCHOOLS
AND TEACHERS WHO
HELP US LEARN FOR
LIFE AND MAKE FRIENDS.

CIAA
WELCOME STUDENTS!
DSCC
CRESTVIEW ELEMENTARY
FCA
COVINGTON HIGH
GO CHARGERS!

GOODNIGHT FESTIVALS
GATHERING US
TOGETHER AGAIN.

COVINGTON

GOODNIGHT FARMERS
WITH FIELDS
BOUNTIFUL AND WHITE.

GOODNIGHT HATCHIE RIVER BOATS CARRYING HUNTERS AND FISHERMEN ALIKE.

GOODNIGHT CHARGER
NATION WHO
CHEERS ON FRIDAY
NIGHTS SO LOUD!

GO CHARGERS!

GOODNIGHT BASEBALL
STATE CHAMPS
MAKING US ALL PROUD!

HOME OF THE TSSAA
BASEBALL STATE CHAMPS
COVINGTON HIGH SCHOOL
1999 * 2006 * 2019

GOODNIGHT PARADES
AROUND THE
SQUARE BRINGING
US SUCH JOY.

COVINGTON
COVINGTON FIRE DEPARTMENT

GOODNIGHT
CHRISTMAS CITY
KEEPING CHRIST
IN CHRISTMAS
FOR EACH GIRL AND BOY.

A Candymaker's Witness
KEEP CHRIST IN CHRISTMAS

GOODNIGHT WATER TOWER
WHO'S STAR SHINES
BRIGHT FOR
ALL TO SEE.

COVINGTON

GOODNIGHT COVINGTON.
GOD BLESS YOU AND
GOD BLESS ME.

MY COVINGTON MEMORIES

DRAW A PICTURE OF YOUR
FAVORITE PLACE IN COVINGTON

Emily Cook is an art teacher, photographer, and the author of "Eclectic Emily" and "Goodnight Covington." She loves discovering the beauty in everyday life. She writes to encourage at **emilypeytoncook.com.**

Lifelong residents of Covington, Emily and her husband, Zach, are enjoying this season of raising their three kids in a small town.

"Eclectic Emily" is available at Amazon.